MW01232215

EDEN'S DAY

by

James E. Hopkins

Dear Serenity,
I hope you enjoy
poetry. It is fun to
read and fun to write.
I hope you will like the
poems I wrote.
Love,
Jim

AuthorHouse™
1663 Liberty Drive, Suite 200
Bloomington, IN 47403
www.authorhouse.com
Phone: 1-800-839-8640

First published by AuthorHouse 1/2/2008

ISBN: 978-1-4343-3262-2 (sc)

Library of Congress Control Number: 2007906659

Printed in the United States of America
Bloomington, Indiana

This book is printed on acid-free paper.

Cover art by Karen Berklund

To Suzan, Zak and Jaleh Therese
A Blessing Without Measure

ACKNOWLEDGMENTS

There are so many people who have touched me and inspired me along the way. It is hard to know where to begin.

Thank you Candy Kramer for being a forever friend and teaching me how to keep the magic in my life. Thank you Anthony Harris, my true soul brother, for inspiring me and giving me the courage to bring all the Itlani material to the light of day. Thank you Magic Circle Dance Theatre (Barbara Gluck, Cecilia Rutkovsky, Dolores Miller) for liberating the dancer in me, for being there always and inspiring my poems and stories. Thank you Harry and Harriet Ortgies for showing me what a life dedicated to the service of Humankind can really look like. Thank you Matt Pasca and Terri Muuss for demonstrating that art, life and spirit are all one iridescent fabric of love. Marc Hensen, thank you for teaching me that perseverance and a truly universal spirit go a long way, all the way to being truly human. Thank you Karen Berklund for sharing your art and support and the beautiful person that you are. Grace and Larry Cardano, your life and living centered on God and prayer fill me with awe and inspiration, thank you. Thank you to the Centering Prayer Group and especially to Barbara Sullivan for being such an insightful soul-friend. Thank you, John Gunter, for inspiring me to always keep on no matter how crazy things seem to get from time to time. Virginia Ziermann, you are looking down from Heaven now but I will always be thankful for learning from you how a life of suffering oppression and abuse can come to good and be a light that shines forever. A very special thank you to Louise Theresa StrongBear, for never letting the shaman light fade and taking us on a grand journey we might otherwise forget.

TABLE OF CONTENTS

BOOK TWO: SPIRIT WAYS

BOOK THREE: ITLANI DREAMS

INTRODUCTION

Giving words wings and letting them take unrestrained flight is what poetry is all about. Language is a sacred, mystical and mysterious thing and although we have lost sight of this it is nonetheless true. Maybe it's about time we get back to that; to letting our words and songs have the power they were born for and reveling in their beauty.

The ancient shamans knew this, the chanters of prayers lived this, healers practiced this. It was not unknown ground to them. It was well traveled territory. Maybe it's time to clear off our dusty passports and once again visit lands of the spirit we have only dreamed of. We can get there and the journey is a soul's beat away, beckoning.

Humankind has always been fascinated with language. For long we have held that the capacity for language was what made us uniquely human. I suspect that the other tribes sharing the planet with us, the animal, plant, and stone tribes, have each their own unique and hidden language known only to them but there is no denying that human language far outstrips any communication system that we know of.

On rays of light our spirits soar high and our hearts burst with what we have to say, want to sing, need to express. Words are our only recourse, the only way we can lay our burdens down, uplift our souls, free our hearts, and share with our human sisters and brothers, what we have learned, suffered, felt, and thought. Words flying through the immensity of space, of the space that we are, into realms only suspected, this is what poetry is all about. There is no heart that has no song, there is no mind that has not thought, there is no soul that does not long for home. That is what poetry is all about. It's not that we are stumped by mystery, confounded by that which is not understood, left out in the cold by ice-fingered enigmas. That is not poetry. Poetry is a reveling in what we do not know but could, in what we have not seen but would, in what we are not yet but could be. Poetry is a world of possibilities that only words on wings can bring us. The door is open, will we not walk through?

Eden's Day is a small sample of what I have to say, want to sing, need to express. In three distinct but related Pathways I have arranged the collection of poems presented here. In Soul Songs the poems deal with the vagaries of life, of meaning, of love, of search, of carrying on and getting carried away. In Spirit Ways are the meditations, prayers, reflections on the flight of the spirit and things we sometimes call spiritual although there is no real separation in the living of it. In Itlani Dreams you will find poems related to the wondrous world of Itlán – a distant, mysterious, amethyst planet somewhere real in our vast galaxy. Some of these poems were written originally in English and some in Itlani. For the Itlani poems English versions have been provided. By these visions I have been truly blessed.

Come along now for an adventure of word-winging, flights of love and wonderment. Don't pack much, you only need what you were born with.

BOOK ONE: SOUL SONGS

SOUL SONGS, the bricks and mortar of everyday life and living. How hard it is to get up everyday, pull on some clothes, arm and shield yourself for the day and head out from home's warm place to hunt or to be hunted. Yet there is subtlety in the Journey. Spirit lurks waiting, surprising us unannounced to bring us back to ourselves, willy-nilly.

Like making a good cheese we try to separate it all out – the curds of life from the whey of spirit. Funny thing though, life won't let us, spirit won't allow it. They're conspiring for us and it's all win-win. Intricately woven, that's life, loose ends and all, yet rich and blessed beyond all understanding.
Despite it all it's good to be alive.

EDEN'S DAY

empathy comes from imagination
so the visionless say
but i was lost in inner space
and saw it a different way.

silence can be useful
so the loquacious say
but i was far from Babel
and heard it a different way.

call on your senses to populate
in this the benumbed hold sway
but i had nothing tactile on
and felt it a different way.

you might think of something you normally shun
so moral this Eden's Day
but i could find no fig for life
and lived it a different way

CLIMBING THE HIGH CEDARS

climbing the high cedars
the views, my soul did jaggedly distress
searching worthy meters
my love, refused so stressingly for less.

following empty leaders
the sight, all temples mercilessly profane
rich food for spirit-feeders
nowhere to escape enthusiasm's bane.

climbing the high cedars
for joy, this light does wonderfully provide
with ecstasy the soul teeters
relief, God's bosom tenderly does hide.

COMMUNION

-for Louise and Nanny, two Angels, one soul

How did it come to pass, I sat there thinking...
That I had gained admittance to this sacred right
For I knew that it was ancient.
So few had witnessed it – fewer still partook.

Tea and cookies – let us raise the holy cup...
Divide love up –
And pass around the Windmill wafers
Awaiting Prophets and other Saviors.

For love so rare – so filled with prayer
Will always sing her Chance
According to the manner of Saint Gregory,
I sat there thinking...

"Tea and cookies," ...the primal texts say
But I knew better...
For Communion never had a name so pure
Or felt so rite.

For I took part and gained new heart
Foretasting the sacred emblems
A living link with Heaven
Or was it Haven...

How did it come to pass,
I sat there thinking.
That I did gain admittance...
How did it come to pass?

COCKROACHES COVERED IN LINDT

-chocolate lovers delight

Beetles will crawl and grasshoppers jump
But when eating a bug it's got to be plump
Of Culinary Insecticide there's hardly a hint
But have you ever had cockroaches covered in Lindt?

DOWN BY THE COLD STREAM

Down by the cold stream
Willow getting stronger
Autumn day is waking now
Night is getting longer.

Gray stone under river's flow
Water tripping lightly
Leaf awaiting winter snow
Woodland swaying sightly.

Bright Star gone a long time
Midweek feeling better
Summer evening's wane aglow
Love a warm fleece sweater.

FALSE LEATHER HAPPINESS

I like the smell of new leather
Not the spirit but the letter
New leather that sweats when it is hot
As time goes by it smells much better.

That sweats when summer's hot
When steam arises from the slumbering streets
After a drenching rain of cloudburst languor.

I'm not sure of it all – not sure
Far away from pith and core
It's false leather happiness
Nothing more.

SPACES

spaces
killing places
of love's interlaces

ever so strong
snow soft, held aloft
of fresh rain, dew, light
sparkling, hiding the darkening

we're going through
fresh new grass, brightly stained glass
of churches old, of spirits new

spaces
without traces
of embraces
for our Life's need

living without braces
for the newborn
struggling seed.

MATER DOLOROSA

For Al Gore

If only someone were listening

I looked into your eyes – deeply blue
How white your hair
How brown your skin
I knew you – distantly – half caring

You fed me, clothed me, sheltered me
In maternal arms – millennia long – you embraced me
Hugged me close – keeping me alive – for better Days
I deserted you – twilight souled – half caring

I heard your cries – saw the flashes of your pain
Felt your trembling – your boils of crimson cleansing
Saw you die – slowly – as acid rain fell upon you
I did not weep – my plans were heavy – half caring

I wandered East – I wondered –
I suspected He would come – would He yet save you?
I would allow no wrinkle upon my convenience
He would be lost – I'd shine no light upon Him – half caring

Look into my eyes – so lifelessly staring
Caress my brown hair – no sign of wisdom latent
Touch my white skin – no warmth beneath the surface
For I was dead long before I killed you –

Mother Earth.

NO NEED

-dedicated to an intense poet, Robert Pasca

the fears of a thousand worlds
spinning around a thousand pulsing stars
scorch our souls filling every nook and cranny
of what we are

no need
find the cool

the heat of a thousand doubts
spinning around our surging spirits
piercing shattered crystal into wounds
of what we want to be

no need
know the cool

the love of a thousand prophets
pouring around our need
filling empty corners left abandoned
of what we've been

no need
touch the cool
taste the cool
live the need

TOWARD THE LIMIT

Stretching toward the limit of good-feeling
To live and know just what to say
To move a small soul's sentiment
To know just how to live cloud-breathing

And so it is with all true friends
A perception of internal strengthening
Finding a world of a little more hope
To leave behind dark shadow-worlds of death.

But somehow I believe these life mysteries
That brilliantly you'll light my way
Carrying sparks of faith to those you love
Abandoning thoughts that bring us salty tears

NOWHERE SEEN

i sailed out to a place nowhere seen before
to ferret the love they said was coming
it was numbing

i had no compass or companion there
only Self and raw construction
soulsong unction

i spied heaven no way guessed afore
soul shards fire-proved but outward craven
i found Haven.

STAY

-for the heroes and victims of 9/11
and those they left behind

It wasn't really like this long ago among the dreams.
Clear was here and I enjoyed it to the marrow.
It stayed with me a long time till perception got too narrow,
When ways got to meandering, abandoning all means.

I really had to stay this and bring it down to peace,
Options soon to leave me on a sudden empty morn.
Ripping out my raw soul, bleeding it to scorn.
Hoping calm would come again and help my sight increase.

It wasn't really like this long ago among the streams
Of confluence and confidence, yet becoming not forlorn,
Of wounds that wound around my fell rejoicing while I mourn
When life set me to wandering and a-wondering

It seems.

TIMBERLINE

In the deep forest, in the dense wood
I breathed you in
Timberline spirit, deep resin of soul
Meaning running down the river's path

Following forlornly forbidden
Looking for the hidden crescent king
Love's domain in barefoot melancholy
Wings taking flight forever free

Soulsore and lonely, longing for release
In the deep forest, in the dense wood
I breathed you in
Timberline spirit, alone and always Thee.

MIST

white cold mist not enough sight
everything shrouded in wraps of light
swaddling clothes of a new born day
seeing where fragments of soul i lay

picking up stones from a bare foot's path
shield over heart in its Godward wrath
i know I should be going but i need to stay
the Road leads me to sowing but i rest to pray

cold white sight what have i missed
where were my lips when my soul was kissed
saving each remembrance with a new found stone
getting back to Carmel sailing out from Rome.

AN ISLAND IS A NAME I KNOW

an island is a name i know
i visit there from time to time
and yet can be a game i show
alone again from see to mime

NEITHER GOODS NOR FAME

Having neither goods nor fame awaiting
Forgetting baubles of my glories past
In oceans deep my wanderings foul abating
Till homeward bound in Haven rest at last.

Shores unseen, unknown beyond soul's sighting
Currents strong, new day's hope soon dashed
Haven's light the lost and lame inviting
My pristine ship so groundedly abashed.

Yet onward still I ply beyond all moorings
Markings left behind, all pathways glassed
Refuge gently calls me on alluring
Abandon I all hopelessness at last.

DRY

desert fathers left me dry
high aground beyond the pale
my life went stale

cloudlike rainshine lit my sky
no rebound outside of Thee
there was no sea

hope that lingers – hear my sigh
hapless sound you would agree
no Thou no me

FALL

gray rain
cold stone
brown wet leaves
empty pavement

wind howls
collar up
feet plod on
feeling tears fall

fall

NEVER

Never so great a light could shine
Never so deep a flow
All of my life's gems to mine
All my raw soul to show

But where would I go?

Seeking for someone to share a heart
Stepping the edge all alone
Knowing beginnings but not where to start
Looking for love where it shone

My life is on loan.

Thinking that this is how it must be
Taking the Path not chosen
Trusting that guidance could only be Thee,
Hoping that soul is not frozen

Or am I just posing?

THE WIND WAS HIGH

salty air, high wind, tossed waves
bones of dead fish upon the shore
purple sand surrounding sea-smoothed stones
awaiting to hide in coming tide

fishermen knee-deep, some boot-high
seabirds searching sustenance diving deep
foam abandoned in the pools left behind
and I awaiting heart, a friend to send

it was i that inside cried
the wind was high, did not bend i

NEGLECTED

The Book of Life was sitting there
Neglected yon afar
I picked it up with dusty hands
Allowed no thoughts to mar

In dark retreat I put it down
It stung – it gave me pause
It brought me to unchartered lands
To wed me to its Cause

I felt so lost, so left behind
No refuge left to take
The pain seared through my mind and soul
My strength began to break

Beyond the place where feelings grow
Abandoned to all shame
I left the Book unopened
Accompanied by pain

I SEE YOU

They abandoned me in "I see you"
Left me to my fate
With all my freight
A heart of gold and veins of blue

Naked in the dark is all I do
Not believing how severe the wait
Till I'm all late
A mind storm-torn for this debate

Let me go beyond the foam
To seas of peace and dove
Beyond the arrows to the love
Where I'll find room and no more roam

ICE-ROSE

it seems as if i've been here before
long before i got here
and now that i've arrived
it's all just memory

it's gentle but it hurts
too many thorns among
the barefoot moss
it's all lost sensory

i've got to get beyond
this ice-rose tundra
and find a climb that's warm
above this storm

DAMSELFLIES

The soil was warm and sweet
The air a golden yellow
Damselflies a-buzzing
Lazy thoughts floating, awhir with life

Purple sweet faint flowers
Entertaining bees and butterflies
Dripping dewlike nectar
Done in trade of future seed

Breezes wafted over my complexion
Feeding spirit softly, impressionist surreality
Garden getting ready for sleep
And I no thoughts to keep

DRONE ON, YOU HATEFUL BORE

-Thank you, Carolyn See

Ah! So nice to see you.
Let me take your coat.
Please have a seat.
Care for a drink? No?

Well then -
Relax -
Start from the very beginning
And tell me everything...

9/11 TAUGHT ME

For Dipti Patel

9/11 taught me

that any given day when I leave for work may be my last on Earth. I should appreciate my loved ones more while I am with them.

that every day when I say goodbye to my loved ones as they leave for work it may be the last time I see them. I should appreciate them more while they are with me.

that any day can be filled with unforeseen dangers, trauma, destruction, or evil.

that any day can be filled with joy, love, caring, and unbelievable heroism.

that our enemies come in many different sizes, shapes, guises and from unexpected places.

that our friends come in many different sizes, shapes, guises and from unexpected places.

that the greatest technologies in the world are not enough to save us.

that God is enough to save us if we let Him.

That Religion can be Humanity's deepest blessing or its greatest curse.

That righteous anger against oppression and injustice is constructive.

That blind, bigoted, bitter, jealous, despairing anger for any reason is destructive.

That big events, either good or bad, can strip away our barriers and unite our hearts and souls.

That small thinking and long held resentments and fears held tightly in the dark can strip away what little of heart and soul we have left.

That God is always close enough to love us and to care when we call on Him in need.

That all too soon we slip back into our heedless sleep of death.

That like Babel, Tall Towers built proudly in the sky can fall and turn to dust.

That small and caring attitudes of love, respect and understanding can reach to the High Heavens.

That I must rise up from my Prison of Self to what it is that God created me to be.

For in the end I can be nothing else and was never meant to be.

And finally 9/11 taught me

That when all is said and done it is still God's World,

And everything we do and are belongs to Him and Him alone.

That is what 9/11 taught me.

I only wish my lessons didn't have to be so hard.

Dipti, I didn't even have a chance to say

Goodbye...

SNOWFLAKE CRISPING

-for Candy, magical adventurer

Snowflake crisping an old brown leaf
Polecat watching in disbelief
Squirrels rasping their long dispute
Oak tree dreaming tall and mute.

Another summer gone beyond
An ice thin layer over pond
An autumn dressed all orange red
Has put all Nature now to bed.

But winter has its charms I know
When ice storms come, set trees aglow
As grey days cleanse us all around
And we find Heaven held aground.

The lanterns glowing from each house
The warmth of homestead to announce
The wonderment of each new sight
All lit by love on winter's night.

RAISE HIGH THE CUP

-for the people of Iraq

Raise high the Cup!
Raise high the Cup!
Heroic deeds have all been done.
The Victor's songs have all been sung.
Raise high the Cup!
Raise high the Cup!

Laid waste to lands once green and fair,
Wide water-songs happily gurgling,
Bright live-alongs forever struggling,
Clouds of rain and new hewn air.

Raise high the Cup!
Raise high the Cup!
Heroic deeds have all been done.
The Victor's songs have all been sung.
Raise high the Cup!
Raise high the Cup!

Brown and scorched our souls do lie,
Remembering outsinged times of nurture,
Regressing to our wound's old suture,
Beneath the stinging tears of Sky.

Raise high the Cup!
Raise high the Cup!
Heroic deeds have all been done.
The Victor's songs have all been sung.
Raise high the Cup!
Raise high the Cup!

IF I SHOULD FALL

If I should fall before you, catch me up,
Leave me not alone without reprieve.
If I should struggle on and drain the cup,
Kiss my lips and eyes before you leave.

RIVERS

Rivers roiling to the Sea
Moths blazing into Flame
And I sit at the feet of Name
Waiting for the Thou of me.

BELOW ITS BEST

nothing seems as careful as it could be
nothing flies beyond the place of tame
each where seems as stale as would be
each one tortures me with torrid game

this betrays enfleshment pure and easy
giving nothing more nor yet received
living death becoming so soul-sleazy
knowing that it's all beyond deceived

i could stay here waiting no how yearning
perceiving that the weight is nowhere guessed
yet i would have the knowledge of this learning
watching as it falls below its best.

BEFORE THE DOOR

I sat there watching as the dew dripped off the leaves,
I hadn't been there in a long time just this way.
The day was warm and pulsing and it slew me as it pleased,
It didn't take a long time – any longer than a day.

The stone beneath my bare feet burning hot among the rays,
I felt a signal lapping of the breeze from off the shore.
No remedy apparent for my distant humming haze,
But this I knew from stone and dew – I sat before the Door.

BASKING

Basking in the warmth of the Eternal One
Light upon light of a resplendent Sun
Seeing without looking, doing till done
Waking more fully to battle unwon.

Veils of splendor clouding my sight
Breathing in waves of Celestial Light
Feeling the tenderness of God's gentle might
Guiding my soul through this perilous night.

When spirit-breathed breezes have calmed my torn soul
And God's sweet scented love has made me whole
When Compassion's bright angels my will have made bold
Then at last I'll have reached my life's light-centered goal.

PHONOLOGY

Of fricatives and plosives and other phonomena,
Linguists take care of those.
I, for this rose, need only nose

As for phonics and their sonics,
What I say goes.
Of fricatives and plosives,
Lord only knows.

An inner ear that strains to hear,
And eyes that long to see,
A soul that tastes its own sweet goal,
That's my phonology.

TIME TRAVEL

Just give me a minute.
I'm not here yet.
I've gotten ahead of myself
And I can't catch up.

You see – I started out living
And hit a speed bump;
Came back to pick myself up
But couldn't find myself.

Didn't have much time,
So I left without me.
And here I am – just
Waiting for myself.

So please,
Just give me a minute.
I'm not here yet.

THE WAY BEFORE ME

-reflections on my conversion

The way before me serpentine and new
The earth beneath my feet both warm and soft
And I without a thought to send aloft
Beneath a sky of white and soulless blue

The way before me pulling ever tight
And I a precious jewel unmined
A shard of heart remaining opaque blind
Realities deeply hidden beyond sight

Bowing head now Godward, new born light
To Garden Paradise long pined
With Lord Bahá my soul-life countersigned
Flowing tears releasing pain's delight

Laying down my burden to walk unbound
The way before me such a gift
Knowing now there's none my soul to lift
But only He Whose Path is Sacred Ground.

LONGING

Sailing across the Shoreless Sea,
Longing for my Lord,
Going alone in search of the One,
My soul became unmoored.

A wave tossed life of pain and love
Soaring so serene,
To reach the beautiful Truth-lit Sun
Beyond all Realms Unseen.

Longing for a Homeland bright,
Straining for the Dove,
Wanting refreshment when Journey is done,
In cool shaded Lands Above.

UNDER WEEPING BEECH TREE

Under weeping beech tree
Safe from all the world
Searching God's lost Mystery
In the darkness curled.

Forgotten and forsaken
So my feelings go,
Soon into light I'm taken
To bask in His warm glow.

TRUTH CHANGES

Truth changes depending on what we know.
Well, there you go –
Blood in the snow –
Waiting till the Spring's well seasoned thaw.

TWO DOORS DOWN

-for Tony and Ron

Two of my friends have fallen in love,
Not far – just two doors down from me,
Tired of being human wannabes.

It's usually not that complicated really.
But they're both from Mars,
Their scars show readily.

How outtuitive life can be when looked at.
Two of my friends have fallen in love,
Not far – just two doors down from me.

YOU TELL ME

Formal or free?
You tell me.
Aren't we all looking for frame
And torture?

Frankly, I don't care mulch.
I would chip away
At my insanity – way outsane for sure.

Formal or free?
You tell me.

OF THE DETONATION OF WORDS AND THEIR COTTONATION

Embracements stagger yet stultify
Away I fly
Never know why
Resting by the wayside

A poet's life on cold windy streets
That know my feet
Feel their repeat
Sighing by the soulside.

Detonation of my words
Never heard
Cottonation in my mouth
Questing at the worldslide.

DISTANT CALL

distant call of high love
beyond the ancient seas
persistent pain of oneness
assuaged not by the breeze

singing songs primordial
to fly celestial ways
stinging longing lovers
recording discordant days

raindrops cold and thirsting
for paths that cannot be
soulblaze set to bursting
beyond the mordant pleas

STINGRAYS SING THEIR SONG

What bright wonder, starfish in a pool of light,
Left behind by ebbing tide, retained for starstruck sight.
How could I have come here, on pilgrimage and free,
Sensing deep disturbance in the ink-black cold I see?

What dark and loathsome waning of a strength that I once found,
Straining for some freedom, now that soul and mind are bound.
Fine sand blowing over broken shells upon the shore,
Taking me beyond myself to sound my inner core.

What might sunder soullife on a lonely isle,
While I tend and nurture it, awaiting new love's smile?
Such a love I feel within, I'll ride this current home
And wash away the darkness with the gentle ocean foam.

Leaving all these thoughts behind I step upon the sand,
Hoping that my starfish bright will straighten up the man.
How could I be left here, alone without a hint,
Of sparklings and glitterings that on the waters glint?

What bright oneness I see here, starlife all around,
Knowing that the Way is sure and that the Journey's sound.
Certain I have come here bringing hope along,
Sitting by the seashore as the stingrays sing their song.

IN THE FOREST OF THE DEAF

in the forest of the deaf
singing bright and strong
dancing for the blind to see
sensations raging long

waiting for an ear to hear
old stories deep and true
waiting for a heart to beat
to see this journey through

so it is in darkness wrapped
in silence still and cold
knowing that the way is long
companions not so bold

away again on lonely course
with freedom joining in
my footfall somehow soothing me
expectant as begin.

COLD MORNING BAREFOOT LOVE

Sands stretching out beyond my sight
Somewhere a crashing sea
Gulls mourning raucously
Cold morning barefoot love

I've been living here alone so long
Sky's dawn returning bringing light
Soul's search leeching out of mind
Cold morning barefoot love

I don't know when I'll leave here
Been alone so long – tears falling saltily
Digging toes among the grains
Cold morning barefoot love

RISING TIDE

It seems not that I could touch the Realm
From whence the subtle scent of native's sage
Did bless.

But I'd have died for less.

A soul evoked so lovingly by gentle fragrant breezes
Unto shores of endless peacefulness unknown.
A dawn above the wave's horizon
Still yet rising.

But I'd have lived for the reprising.

It seems I could not bide the gale
Nor tell this tale beyond a sea of my own making;
Everything forgiven, nothing taking.

But I'd have stayed among the wisps
Of clouds, and waves, and spirit breaking.

Walking Lonely Path beyond all measure,
Unknown ways of Sage and Treasure.
It seems indeed that only I could guide the Helm
Beyond the Rising Tide of my Forsaking.

JOURNEY LONG

The Song of the Camel Cricket Caravan

-for Grace and Larry

Camel crickets journey long
Over Sand and Dune,
Leaving Homeland far behind
To find Warm Refuge soon.

Coming in through Jagged Cracks
To brighter Realms of Play,
To join the Native's living there
Extending Winter Stay.

Camel Crickets journey far
Both under Sun and Moon.
They'd like to join your family too –
A cold night's Winter's Boon.

TIGER AND THE SERPENT

Tiger in the jungle
Serpent in high grass
I look out beyond horizons
Dark with clouds.

Feet planted firmly on the ground
Naked to the pulse of foreign world
Heart beating strongly, soul afire
And I yet roam.

Tiger and the Serpent
Take me home
No more to taste the salt
Of tears alone.

THAW SHE GOES!

-melting icecaps
global warming
nobody listening

Yaks and cats and flittering bats,
Up to Mount Everest so high.
I have to go up! I have to go up!
For Long Island is no longer dry!

Up on the mountain as far as you go,
Up on the mountain so free.
I've got to go up! I've got to go up!
For Long Island is covered by sea!

Yaks and cats and flittering bats,
High in Tibet we will be.
We're staying up high! We're staying up high!
So dry and so cozy, you'll see!

I'D LIKE TO LEAVE NOW

It seemed so real when I first got here
A luminosity pure – suffusing
But then it got confusing.

Rude and crude was all I found
Then I got bound
All connection celestial – defusing

I got stained beyond repairing
Thoroughly pained beyond real caring
Nothing sparing

I think I'd like to leave now.

DAWN CAME

dawn came breaking over the horizon
sleepy villages paid no heed at all
morning mist dissipated – nature stirred
slumberers heavy headed restless in their beds.

new light on old and darkened ways filled with dust
stone and craggy earth crusted dry and lifeless
a few children waking up – squinting into the bright sky
others dream in silent oblivion unconcerned with the New Day

dawn came breaking over the horizon
sleepers moving off to find the dark and cool
birds flew free – vast widening heavens open to their gaze
leaving sleepers heavy-deaded in their beds

PLOD ON

Frosty clinkling silver bells
In the sudden moonlight
Illumining the Path and Sacrifice
Step by step plodding on – air so still.

Night fragrance – heavy honeysuckle
Summer's night's warmth surrounds
Dust and sweat in soul's deep recesses
Burden long carried without respite.

I want to sit and rest awhile
Drink and revive a heart long thrashed
No more be weary along this Gem-lit Path
But so it will not be – plod on.

MARBH LE TAE

"Marbh le tae, marbh gan é."
That is what they tell me most every day.
It's sweet but oh so green and I...
I'm from the streets of Heartworn.

Damned if you do, damned if you don't,
Taking another sip I say.
The stones are cold here and I've a long way.
"Marbh le tae, marbh gan é."

As the Irish say...

RAIN FELL GENTLY

-I am still remembering you, Ginni

The rain fell gently on our friendship
Running rivulets down the bookshop window
Sipping coffee over French magazines and biscuits
Life had never been so good, so simple.

A gray day to the many and the busy
Hustling and bustling over many cares
I watched them knowing I had something better
Dry and warm in friendship's glow.

You are gone now, taking flight in skies unknown
Tears running rivulets down my soul
No more bookshop reveries in the gentle rain
Life had never been so good, so simple.

WESTERING SUN

Deep within the fibers of my woven self
The orange-yellow warmth spread out
Relaxing mind and soul in soft release
Putting down, in respite, loads long carried.

Come morn I will take them up again
At birds' bright greetings – new born light
But that is another day's path – not yet taken
Deep within the fibers of my woven self.

SWEET WATER

Such a sweet gentleness
Water on stone backsplashing
Cool, refreshing self-imagination
Walking the stone slippingly.

Fragrant green moss
Awaiting Benediction's sprinkle
And the soft fresh touch
Of a solitary Barefoot Wanderer.

Sweet water's mist
In the eyes of a beholder
Reluctant yet unblinking ever so
Cultivating soullight sunshine.

THIS VAST EXPANSE

It is not that I have not understood this vast expanse
Or that I lost my way in its beginnings.
It's just that I did not care to dine at trivialities
On a shore that others would not swim.

I plunged in – waist deep – the soft bog capturing me
No struggle but a realization of suffocating richness.
Knowledge beyond comprehension – heart beyond emotion
It's just that I did not care to speculate among the dead.

This vast expanse! Why does it call me – soft, embracing,
Taking away all breath as if beyond the needs of its own making?
I have not lost my way in its beginnings although
Pathless is the Way that it engenders – unmarked journey.

I have struggled in this net – entangled, abandoning all love.
The dead sang nothing in the blackness that I would hear.
Wisdom arrived beyond self realization leaving me burnt and blistered.
It's not that I have not understood this vast expanse.

LIKE A JOEY

The multiplex of your thoughts left me far behind
Although I knew you minced no words.
Like a joey hidden in your mother's pouch your mind
Had zero tolerance for greeting the light of day.

But that was my gold mine, my hidden trove
I could not compromise with your marsupial
Hiddenness so adroitly tucked away.
It's simple really, this affair of heart.

MAGICAL FEELING

Inspired by Cirque du Soleil

Love thunders into our lives
Awakening us to possibilities
And the light we carried so long alone
We join to others – there is safety in numbers

Caught up in this storm
We spin our new realities
Members of a new born pack
Seeking what we did not have

Love strengthens our living
And then like a vapor in the desert
Dissipates like a traceless perfumed scent
Of who we have become.

This is Love's Way.
What a magical feeling.

OSPREY

Proud perched osprey blessing my island home,
As a boy I watched your high flight overhead
Where lone and strong your life song pulsed
And summer its languid soul pushed forward towards its goal.

If it were not so I would have guessed,
For I was a precocious boy set up to knowing.
On my island I so lived – left dry and underheard
Where I did sing defending from this sting – flying.

Now you are back bringing memories,
As I singing remember who I was and how –
Hope's bright flight would walk me home from school,
Grasshoppers scurrying underfoot asphalt Armageddon.

MONOGLOTTERY

You've got one tongue
I've a few
Breathing as a human
Just one won't do.

Pay attention to the words
This is what I say
They lumber on in ancient herds
Looking for a soul or two.

Translations and synopses come our way
Seething past the swarm
We've got too few that really do
Beyond the wordsmith's form.

Verbal insight is required
Look around and see
We've got just us
Word-warming, you and me.

THIS I SEE

Years have fallen off my tree
Yet this I see
Cold and dark wet leafless plains
Where once rain splashed gray slated stone
I walk barefoot all alone.

In the distance on soul's shore
A fire of the hearth or heart
A new beginning soon to spark
Rising to a life unknown
Where I kneel naked once more home.

BY CHOICE

Light dripping from the fence beams
Held by globes of rain
And I my pain –
Sitting in the afternoon beglazed
Waiting for the meaning of these days.

Could it be it's all about this sojourn
To see if peace will come again and stay the night
I could have it other ways by choice
But given feeble sight
I'll hold my voice from this delight.

FLYING FREE

This blinding light is all I see
Veils upon veils, beyond beyond
Yet this is my longing, my only bliss
For I would lonely miss if not for Thee.

Call me up to Haven's Rest assured
For there is no other refuge I would go to
I have seen enough of sea and clay
To Thee and Thee alone is my heart moored.

Tired of the burden so long carried
Piercing now the light that hides Thy face
Abandoning a life that stung and harried
Flying free now to Thy Sacred Place.

WIDE OPEN

I sat among the Dust Collection
Old pages cracked open wide like the hearts that bled them
I wondered, "What was it all for?"
"Could we have forgotten before the ink had dried?"

No assuaging this pain I knew
Old stories retold in hope's new found despairing
I wondered, "Was anyone there when they cried?"
"Or was all abandoned cut and die?"

I'll just shelve this now; there's nothing for it.
My archeology doesn't run that deep
Someone perhaps will visit once again
Old pages cracked wide open; lost the loves that fed them.

TEAPOT

The teapot sitting there
All white porcelain – a gold skin thin and sheer
Sweet water-born aromas wafting
On the wings of curling steam.

Ah! Once again in Orient's embrace
Basking in long memories of Cathay
Sipping soul's sole solace through burnt lips
Putting down the fragile cup – alone.

POTTER'S CLAY

Potter's clay, carpenter's wood,
It's all about might; it tells of how should.
I've nothing in it.
Creator did spin it.

Mason's stone, scribe's dark ink,
It's all in life's rugbies of maybes and could bes.
Could I yet win it?
Saint it or sin it?

Perhaps I'll just float it
And not let myself sink.

BOOK TWO: SPIRIT WAYS

SPIRIT WAYS, the sweet Paths of Love and Light beyond all words, beyond all labels, beyond all feelings we can express. The Life Path from spirit birth to worlds of Eternal Wonderment that only the Soul knows as Home. Bathing in the Splendor of the Divine. Basking in a Love as yet not recognized. Finding our true Haven at last where nothing of this world can touch us but everything is touched by a Radiating Caring beyond all reckoning.

MY HEART'S PARADISE

MEDITATION OF A UNIVERSAL SOUL

O God! You have brought me to this place and here I am. Naked. You are the only Love of my life although I have tried lesser loves. I looked for You everywhere and did not find You. I neglected You and found You everywhere. It is You I want – without borders. I rest in You – beyond all labels. No doctrines hold me. No forms entangle me. You are without form and formless is my love for You. You are my Heart's Paradise.

I see You in the Law of Moses, I feel You in the Love of Jesus. In the Play of Krishna You are there and in the Wisdom of Buddha. I see You in the Peace of Muhammad, in the Purity of Zoroaster and in the Splendor of Bahá. And yet – I do not see you but in the quiet of my heart. You are my Heart's Paradise.

Like the Wind You give me freedom. Like the Earth, stability. Like the Water You purify me. Your Fire burns away my darkness. You alone are the Pearl of Great Price. You alone are the Jewel in the Lotus. You alone are Whom I seek. You are my Heart's Paradise.

You sent Your Law to protect me and your Love to save me. You offered your Play to cheer me and Your Wisdom to guide me. You gave me Your Peace to humble me and Your Purity to refresh me. Into my heart You have cast Your Splendor. You are my Heart's Paradise.

Knock on the Door of my heart and give me grace to let you in. Stay with me and give me strength to hold You dear.

You are my Heart's Paradise!

BLACK PIT

-dedicated to the Prophet Bahá'u'lláh

Down the steep stairway into the Dark
The Light was bright-shining, the contrast was stark
The Beloved of Ages sitting in filth
The world was awaiting the Loved One's bright mark.

Chants were ascending in melodious tones
Above all the murmurs, the whimpers, the moans
For Light was now rising to flood all the world
Beyond the starvation, stained rags and dried bones.

And now farthest reach of sea, desert or plain
Is bathed in His love, taking all of our pain
The Promised One shattering all prison walls
Has washed Mankind clean of indelible stain.

Peace beyond measure, unbridled and sure
The weeping and suffering will hound us no more
Bahá'u'lláh's Arising awaited so long
Has opened each heartway, each Heavenly Door

So let us sing praises to the Ancient of Days
And learn of His wonders and follow His ways
Beauty so blessèd has filled deep our souls
Delivered us all from hate's darkening maze

Bringing us all to Love's brightening Days...
Bringing us all to Love's brightening Days.

**The Prophet Bahá'u'lláh, Manifestation of God on Earth, Uniter of our hearts and of the Planet itself, received His Divine Mission in 1853, in the Siyah Chal, the Black Pit of Tehran – a pestilential dungeon that gave birth to the Light that illuminates the World*

BASKETS FULL LEFT OVER

-to Jesus of Nazareth and His cousin John

How could loaves and fishes change the world?
And one lone locust-eater shed tears no one would see?
How could it all depend on Me?
That out of Egypt's darkness Love was hurled.

And I, before the people, God's sustaining Word,
Pillar of Light beyond the cloud,
The still small Voice forever loud,
That marshals stars and galaxies and each small bird.

I've come to feed them, give them what I know,
New visions for the soul beyond the Tree.
Such is My goal to end there, yet to be
With My true Father where none else can go.

Will they remember that I am the Son
That fed them all beyond My sorrow's pain
And baskets full left over yet remain
When on the Tree My sweet Life's Journey's done?

TO POPE JOHN PAUL II THE GREAT

How could we have ever guessed
Light upon light in Splendor dressed
Ascended from a Land of Slavic East
Thereby a tortured world so hell-bound blessed?

How could we have ever seen
The captain of our souls destroy the beast,
To show us Heaven in a cloudless dream
Beyond the mediocre and the mean?

For Heaven reached down in you to give its best
And Man through you rose to heights unseen.
The dark-souled sword malignant pierced your breast,
Taking our world beyond, in tortured Quest.

For this we know, now darkened, as foreseen,
The soul shone white, the body outward worn.
Its rays of love and perseverance gleam
Throughout a Universe of hearts, your gifts to glean.

And so to you John Paul we say goodbye,
Praying in Spirit's patience not foresworn,
Guide us ever on your Path of Love,
And bless Mankind with your compassion's eye.

CHRISTMAS NIGHT

I looked beneath the Christmas tree
To see what love I'd find,
To taste the gifts and treasures there,
Their qualities and kind.

And peeling back the layers
Of the Season's greed and din,
I found a Child of Light and Love,
Who took away all sin.

Luminous gems were hidden between
The tinsel and the gaud,
Looking for what I could not see,
I found our Loving Lord.

I looked beneath the Christmas tree
Both heart and soul unfurled,
And this I learned on Christmas night:
A God-Child lit the world.

Christmas 2004

FOOTPRINTS IN THE SNOW

The footprints in the snow I followed all alone,
They took me far and distant, but it felt like going home.
I followed in my tattered clothes, it chilled me to the soul,
It seemed like warmth had come alive my sadness to console.

And the people were astonished by the brilliant Nighttime Star,
There was talk of distant visitors come to see it from afar.
They say a Prophet came to Earth born upon the hay;
It felt like love descended and peace had come to stay.

And there among the farmhands and the beasts, lain upon the grass,
A Child of Light and Wonderment His earthly time to pass,
Had come to fill the world with love and teach us all the Way.
It felt as if the tears were gone where angels came to play.

I bowed my head unto the ground, tears fell upon the dirt.
I felt the burden lifted as He took away my hurt.
A Child of Love and Mercy had made the world complete.
It felt as if my life began as my fears fell at His feet.

The footprints in the snow I followed to my Home,
They took me near unto my Lord where endless Light outshone.
I followed in royal robes this time, my soul's new love entire,
From lowliness and loneliness my Lord had called me higher.

And the people were astonished that the King was born so low,
But I followed lonely footprints in the frozen winter snow.
More than a Prophet came to Earth to set all Mankind free,
But miracle of miracles, He came to care for me.

Christmas 2005

I REMEMBER CHRISTMAS

-Thank you, Aunt Grace, for the Christmas lantern.

Thinking back to years past
When Christmas was a jewel,
When childhood filled my eyes with light
And life was not so cruel.

Remembering how the snow felt
On my cheeks so full of life,
When bright stars shining in the night
Knew neither war nor strife.

Praying for a new world
Based on Love and Peace,
Where justice lives in every home
And calls for hate to cease.

How bright the colored lanterns
Reflected on the snow,
Remembering Christ's Birth in my soul
Where only God would know.

Marveling at the love-wrapped gifts
That told of Peace on Earth
Bathing in a Love Divine
Where God in Man took birth.

Christmas! What a miracle
Of Love And Peace so mild!
I feel it now all over again
As when I was a child.

For God's love is an ageless love
Beyond all we understand...
Feeling the warmth of Christmas again
In God's true Love for Man.

Christmas 2006

FRENCH MONASTERY SOUP

Enjoying some French Monastery Soup
Eating it right up in a silent group
Soon you'll find it's becoming quite a habit
And after all there's no other way to have it.

Preparing yourself, you've really got to try it
Centering your soul in the Monastery quiet
Soon you'll learn it's all about the Inner
Give it all to Him whether saintly or a sinner.

So if this is a life to which you will aspire
Eating your soup here in bliss among the friars
Come aside tranquilly to cell of wood and stone
Dining with the One True God and never quite alone.

MONASTERY CAT

Living in the belfry
Listening to the bats
Floating on the plainsong
Away from other cats

Scurrying with the friars
To sing my morning prayer
Running past the briers
Through gardens kept with care

Stealing from the pantry
Forgiveness sure to come
God's presence in a Lantern
Just knowing He's the One

A monastery cat is what I am
My spirit warm and free
Savoring a life that only I can
A cat among monks I'll be!

BROKEN BELL

-for George Gerardi and his Nepali bell

Broken bell and broken heart,
Lonely wanderer to do his part,
Calling slumberers to awake
And in God's silence to partake.

Broken heart and broken bell
Secrets of the Journey tell.
Waiting for the morning sun
When God's true work is gently done.

Yearning for the Primal Word,
When only quiet can be heard,
Where souls in veils of light rejoice
Beyond the Promise and the Choice.

O ANCIENT BEAUTY, HOW I NEED...

O Ancient Beauty, how i need You to come and take up residence in my heart. I am alone in the Dark, guide me to the One of Light. It has been so long, salám, since i left the Holy Place, take me back to the Mashriqu'l-Adhkar of my Heart. Cleanse me with Your Hand of power. Give me back to myself.

There is only You
Source of all sources
Revealer of all Light

Bahá, Bahá, Bahá
O Ancient Beauty
How i need You

Don't leave me in the Dark
Give me back to myself
Don't leave me...
Don't leave me... alone

**Ancient Beauty is a title of the Prophet Bahá'u'lláh, Founder of the Bahá'í Faith*
***Mashriqu'l-Adhkar, the Dawning Place of the Remembrance of God, is a universal Temple of Divine Worship.*

O THOU BAHÁ

O Thou Bahá, O Thou Lord and Savior! Bringer of Delight to every Heart. Cleanse Thou my sight. Heal Thou my aching soul. Take Thou me to Thy lofty Goal. Leave me not alone... it is so cold.

I need Thee more than life!
For that Thou art.
With Holy Breath fill Thou me
So that I may live.

I need Thee.

O Thou Bahá, come unto me, dwell within me now.
The Walk is long.
The Way is cold.

Take me to the One!
For that Thou art,
Manifest on Earth.
Leave me not alone... it is so cold.

WARRIOR'S STAFF

I have taken up the warrior's staff, lead Thou my Way.
O Perfection Blessed, give me rest, the Battle knows
no respite and i am far from Home. Far from Thy
Sacred Throne.

Such is the Way of the Warrior.
My soul's flight of ceaseless search
My heart aching for the One Companion, aching for
a Way paved with jewels of holiness, a blessing to
all Wayfarers such as we. Other ways we cannot see.

O Perfection Blessed, millennia have passed since i first
left Thee. Take me back. Give me to myself as whole
i was. I have taken up the warrior's staff. Guide
me in the Way that I must go.

Plunge me into Thine Oceans of Purifying Light.
Hold my heart within Thine Own.
Leave me not alone...

**Perfection Blessed (Blessed Perfection) a title of the Prophet Bahá'u'lláh, Founder of the Bahá'í Faith.*

GOLD

O Lord Bahá, i have seen Thy dawning Light.
The Light dawning in my heart. It warms me. It
warms me like liquid gold. Keep me close to Thee.
Warm and safe.

The glowing horizon from whence Thy love is rising calls
to me, calls me home, home where i feel safe and
secure. The warm flowing golden Light of Thy love
embraces me, surrounds me, reassures me, hugs me
close.

i am home again warm and safe.
Home again sitting by the fire,
Sitting by the Hearth of Thy warming golden Light.
The Light that Lights up the World. The liquid Gold
that warms all worlds – both the visible and
those not yet seen.

i thank Thee.
Thou hast not left me alone
And cold in the Dark.

NAKED

The green and fragrant plain stretches out before me.
The emerald grass moist beneath my bare feet as i walk
naked.

Naked like the Warrior's son.

i have never known him who sired me nor she who bore me.
Bless them both in realms eternal as in Worlds below,
The green and fragrant plain stretches out before me.
Naked, i will perhaps one day find them...

Find them in finding Thee... the true Source.
The emerald grass moist beneath my bare feet.
As i journey walking,
Walking back to Thee.
Back home,
Back home to Thee.

Warm
Safe
Secure

PULSE

The drums keep beating, i feel their pulse, i see
the waves of Light birthing from Mother Earth crying
out to Heaven... Father Sky

Shaman knows
Spirit flows
Thy Light grows

i wrap the Blanket around me against the Cold.
i keep close to the Light of Thy Warmth, for life itself.
Chants bubble from within, the bells on my ankles
herald Thy coming Love as i dance. As i dance the
circle... shaman way.

Fly Thou my spirit into the Light.
Give Thou me true sight.
Protect me through this Night.

Thou art my Friend,
Leave me not alone...

LIGHT

O Bahá! i want You! Let me pull up my anchor,
hoist my sails and start on my way home to
You.

Like an explorer thirsting for a new land where
all is Love, i sail to You... Shelter me in the
new found harbor of Your Love. On my way home
sailing upon Your Oceans of Light, i want You.

Waves of Light surround me; in the distance,
shimmering isles of tenderness beckon and call my
soul. Shelter me there, for i have been too long
alone – the journey too long, the way too arduous.

Sailing Seas of Light on my way home to You
Joy fills me up – i am safe and strong,
healthy and loved, a radiating star in the
firmament of You!

Light, Light, Light, Light.

TEACHER

O Lord Bahá! Thou art my Teacher. I bow down
and kiss the hem of Thy robe… tears streaming
down my face.

I have been so long away.
Help me this time to stay.
To be totally Thine just this one day.

Teach me what i long to know… guide me on my Way.
Open up the portals of my heart.
Help me make a start.

Returning home to Thee… as is my Quest.
Eternal Peace and my soul's Rest.
Flood me with Thy Light in this Dark Night.

O Lord Bahá! Thou art my Teacher.
Rebellious student though i be.

Stay with me.

I HAVE RETURNED

i have returned...
i have returned to my people
The Lovers of Bahá, bathing in the Light
Beyond All-Sight.

My heart's yearning, pain so sweet.
Love's flame...
Can't take this heat... True Love
To Meet.

O my own True Lover. Stay with me close.
Wrap Your Crimson Robe around my aching bones.
Bring the Chalice of Strength to my parched lips.
Help me to drink...
Before i sink.

Help me up, Your hand in mine.
I am all Your Own. Keep me close,
Your hand in mine.

POOL

Sparkling pool, shimmering and fair
Cool and clear, deep and pure. Sparkling pool...
The pool of Thy never-ending Love. i bow to
Drink.

O Lord of Light and Beauty! Let me walk in
Thy Company... Angels lifting me up as i
Stumble.

Sparkling pool – in Thy refreshing purity let me
Swim...
Swim into Thine arms. Wrap Thy Light around me...
Keep me safe and warm...
In the Warmth of Thy Love.

With Thy Light in my heart
i will strive to do my part
In Thy cool and sparkling pool.
Angels lifting me...
As i sink.

RHYTHM

O Magnificent One! O Thou Radiating Light of
Eternal Love!
Wave after wave engulfs me... the Rhythm of Thy
Sea... now me.

The drops know no peace beyond the Shore.
i long for more.
Slave after slave the Chains release
And so learn Peace.

O Radiant Beauty beyond All-Sense! O Thou
Loving Eternity, Magnanimity Immense! No peace
is there such as Thine... now mine.

In Thine Ocean let me Be.
In Thy Radiance let me See.

Waiting on the Shore
No more.

BOOK THREE: ITLANI DREAMS

Most of the ITLANI DREAMS (ta Talmenshunú Itlana) were originally written in the language of the Itlani who, although of Earthly provenance, long ago before the Age of Cataclysms migrated to another world yet still in our own Milky Way and so they are accounted an alien race, yet they are our cousins.

Of how I came to know of the Itlani and their ways, culture, and language is not a story to be told here. Of the many stories and poems found in the *Firefoot Chronicles* few have as yet been translated into English. The translation of the most inspiring of these stories, *The Enchantress of Djanár,* the soul thrilling history of Pulán-Shuv's push toward Itlani Unification, is well on its way to completion.

The discovery of these tales and how I came to work on them is an inspiring story some day to be written but it has released in my soul many a wordsong some of which I share with you here.

DINI VEY MUNKA

"Inside and Out"

Ode to Itlán

-to Péyus, my Itlani brother

O my remembered yet forgotten world,
Lavender, orange, bejeweled sunset reverie,
Sweet smell of desert flower love,
Cool air iridescent butterflies on the khará and stone.

How I long to see you once again,
To breathe your still sweet warmth and scent
Drinking in the peace you're known for,
Waiting for the moons to pave my path.

Calling you to mind, my sweet Itlán,
Wanting once again to feel your touch,
Naked and alone in your embrace,
O my forgotten yet remembered world.

**Khará is a succulent cactus-like plant growing in the deserts of Itlán known for its powerfully fragrant yellow and orange blossom.*

MABUGAY TA KARESE

"From Beginning to End"

An alien mind
A body of Earth
And of understanding a doleful dearth
From beginning to end: a mis-hewn birth.

Siarelian find
Abandon Itlán
And going beyond my own Star Path's plan
From beginning to end no well sewn man.

A minstrel's rind
Yet piercing its juice
Seeing within beyond all foreseen use
In both worlds attuning to Tamú's sweet Muse.

**Siarél is the Itlani name for Earth. Tamú is one name the Itlani have for the Creator.*

TERRAN STAR

-To Suzan, my Dral-Vul

I'm looking out across the far flung western sky,
The setting Sun of Terra's golden yellow fading light.
But cool refreshing evenings of my homeworld make me cry,
For to return to sweet Itlán seems so beyond my might.

How gentle were the breezes of the deserts far and wide,
How fresh the warm soft sand beneath my naked feet.
How sweet the crags and crannies where desert blossoms hide,
And I a wandering warrior my own true love did meet.

The beautiful Dral-Vul I found one day at river's edge,
A-washing scented hair among the willows and the stones.
As she gathered up her few small things from off the flowered hedge,
I knew true love at first sight from the aching of my bones.

But she I left so long ago to journey out in space,
And on another pearl-blue world so sadly made my home.
So ne'er again will I cast a glance on my beloved's face,
As I watch the Terran Star go down on a new world now my own.

TA UBUPRÓN TA KOYA

THE LAMENT OF THE SNOW

Kesh dralizhe mishyana ha?
Kesh zhoyese kadimyazha da?
Djurova tsorni mampisyanu.
Ta rozhova zhanya rinkasyanu.

Would anything go well?
Will I gain understanding?
I would seek it now.
I would dance to find my peace.

Iküí ta dralan kadimyata ha!
Telyus djama samyata ra!
Rinkas ta reza alyara khaá,
Daova ta mampisa tebyanu zhoy-sá.

May something come from all this good!
Banished be the taste of evil!
Serenity's dance of such worth,
I myself would hold the understanding of this Search.

Idaizhe mishyara zhoyit nikh.
Djemarizhe tarshyara ta etíkh.
Vey rahaova lafiyanu zhoy...
Ranti lokhyana iidit koy.

So goes my soul.
Suspicion full grows.
And I have nothing...
When this snow falls.

Var ta koy kalova fulatsyana,
Vey ta nikh shtadaatsyana,
Kiinizhe seti shey karisan.
Ta koyrinkasa nikhgarisa.

The snow would bring trust,
And the soul would understand again,
As it is at every small ending.
This snowdance of my soul's pain.

DINI TIKARIAN

IN TICARY

Iíz mashrá franarit gleyavá djanubyaru,
Ta ketashú ta shatuna badakashit inu.
Zhoyit talshú seti ta maban zhoyit varemira,
Garís ta zakha ta nikhova khisyara.

I have been sitting here for hours,
The sounds of the city far distant.
My thoughts on the breast of my love,
A pang of the heart stabbing the soul.

Ta dozulú karyiven zhe, ta shatardja dozhakyara,
Suú dini nuzhit kamsaavá vozdozhilisa tukbelyaren.
Vey sundjit tansubyaru zhoy basheysha ishvemarizhe
Kinzaese bashit varemós zhoyesha kreykunyana.

The rains have just ended, the city drips,
Children in wet shirts play at puddles.
And naked I stand without you wondering
Where your love could have wandered without me.

Chayyara ta shatún rumbi ta dozulan,
Zhoyit nikh iíd silova peyratyara.
Ta garís franartantoilu kiarayara.
Ta ketashú ta shatuna badakashit inu.

The city smells sweet after the rain,
My soul accepts the loss.
Long the pang in my heart sleeps,
The sounds of the city far distant.

*Ticary (Tikari) is an ancient Itlani city of scholars and philosophers. It is also the home of Tsiasuk-Pron, the author of this poem, who works at the Ticary Institute, *ta Istonza Tikaria*, for the Itlani Language Academy.

KHARAIT TALORSABÚT

CACTUS SUNRISE

Ta chayit seylár ta ananarun zhoyit malachuda,
Seti ta khalavá ta ilazoit Givanuna.
Zhigutú zhoyese haova ruvya makayaren ra aréy
Ruzay ta seylarova bashit varema tsalyavu ratá.

The sweet scent of the flowers of my youth
At the borders of the vast open Desert.
Rememberings can no longer tell me anything
But I have never forgotten the fragrance of your love.

Ta skaz bashit blikhnorga dudj zhoyan seti harkazavá
Ta franarit vey sundjit tuurosa mogit nikharun,
Ta inurovinós mogit tayamalatsit shagalarun,
Ta penkér bashit shona vey ta telyus bashit kunzaya.

The smell of your body against mine during night
Of the new and naked penetration of our souls,
The wandering pilgrimage of our fleeing minds,
The clove of your sweat and the taste of your skin.

Idá zhoyova shastendayafyara u dini ta rozhan
Fazhenit untara ta nikhreza salaya makayatu,
U bashit penkeratsit seylár zhoyay branyana ratá,
Mu blikhnorg, mu nikh - maronyari sheytá.

It relaxes me that in the peace
Of a new world of tranquil soul I might sleep,
That your clove-like scent would never leave me
One body, one soul – we will always be each other.

SATÉL TALMENSHUNEK

SHAMANESS

Klaná ta Naavá dzevunyavel,
Mishbatovó ta nikha zhanshunarizhe.
Vuyinova dralizhe pilayaru, dzevovó loshkorunyavi,
Talmenit shunenovó loshshunyavi seti kadayan.

Across the Great Grasslands she journeyed,
Discovering Pathways of the soul.
I know her well, we have traveled together,
Thirsty we have seen visions together.

Mantayaven ta dzarú, giliryaven ta oznatú, ruzay
Razhgerit ta nikhú var Uramún mogeylo setiramyavad.
Ta Sitinún piti mogit mishbatan sheyova chayavor.
Ta mishú shtakimsiafyaven vey shprunafyaven kha.

The mountains were high, cold the rivers, but
Our souls were warm for the Great Friend walked with us.
The Great Star above our way watched all things,
Refreshing our goings and strengthening them.

Gadanlirek onyarel, pronár ta pronarun, dafarár ta dafararun.
Iidova ishyavu, shunyavu, dekuvayyavu.
Sheyú diváy vuyinan uvakunilu ba vleseyrizhe fidiripronyaren,
Shey ramfél chayyit biráf onyara.

She is a Wordwinger, a singer of songs, a giver of gifts.
This I have known, this I have seen, have experienced this.
All things around her, strong-voiced but sweetly sing out their song,
Each footstep a sweet scented adventure.

Zhoyit zurhanél ta talmena, satél talmenshunek.

My spirit-sister, the shamaness

**Great Friend: Uramún or Great Friend is the most often used Itlani name for the Creator.*
***Wordwinger: Itlani word for poet; a person who gives wings to words and sets them free to fly with the spirit.*

TA ONARIT RAHÁ

THE NOTHING

Rahaskatán onyaru vey shassopiit khaá.
Teynikadimyava rapá vey zaridéyn ta murnnikhuda tsiryara,
Ruzay samyara ta onós vey stranyaru zhoy.
Rahaska rozhit ardja onyara vey djamó sheyan anarakyaru.

I am a citizen of Nowhereland – directionless.
No one came. This life of loneliness burns.
But being remains and I am rich.
Nowhere is a peaceful realm and beyond it all I am content.

Ta mampisós karivit onyara, ta seyón dayiva kha,
Ta murnúd zhoyova rekhtayyara shas u ishyata hapá.
Koelivit hazbatú sundjramilisa mishyavu – rahaova zhanavizhe,
Ruzay ta rozhós loshmishyava var shprunit samyavu.

Seeking is over, the fruits understood,
Aloneness follows me without anyone knowing.
Barefoot I walked the moonlit paths – finding nothing,
But peace walked with me for I stayed strong.

Kiinit imár ta rahaatsa! Kiinit dakivúl ta murnuda!
Ta tsirtsír razhgeyrisyazha vey keylidzevyazhu zhoy sheytá.
Ta onarit rahá zhoyit uramór izmui.
Ta onarit rahá uramór zhoya khaá.

What a taste of nothingness! What a dark brown soil of solitude!
The fire will give warmth and I will journey on forever.
The Nothing is my true lover.
The Nothing my lover indeed.

GAZHÓN ANANA

EXILE OF A FLOWER

ta seylár bashit ananarun gozyava
vey bashova inuovatyavi
ta bandjinova peyratya ra-makayavi
ubuún ta durumuda piti sheyan daryava

the fragrance of your flowers irritated
and we pirated you away
we could not accept your beauty
a great dark sadness lorded over everything

dini meyladjan bashova samafyavi
reshú bashit setión raizhe chegyata
reshú bashit ananovó shunya ra-cheykopyati
dini ta durumese bashova gazhonyavi

we exiled you to your prison
so that your presence would not touch us
so that we would not have to witness your florescence
into the darkness we exiled you

ra-vemyaru u zhoyit nikh ardakiyata
var ta dral inubonduivit onyara
reshú rapá seti bashan yavyoyata
dini ta bashlaan inu ta seylaray basha.

i don't want my soul to spoil
because beauty has been hidden away
so that no one will rejoice with you
in the silence far away from your sweet scent

HOME AGAIN

cool desert sunset
sands no longer burn
small dune denizens delight
i am home again on sweet itlán.

fresh breeze brisk and sweet
hair swept from my face i stop
and find that somehow hence i never left
for i am home again on sweet itlán.

look out to the orange purple orb
horizon reaching up for its embrace
rising moons beam love-rays on my face
for i am home again on sweet itlán.

Printed in the United States
200993BV00008B/130/A

9 781434 332622